GETTING PROMOTED

First published by Advantage Quest Publications edition issued by arrangement with the author. Revised by the author in 2021.

Advantage Quest Publications is an imprint of Advantage Quest Sdn. Bhd. (320311-T)

For information regarding the 2021 online publication, contact the author directly at davidjhirst@yahoo.co.uk

Print version distributed in Singapore by Advantage Quest Pte. Ltd. 200905563N)

Originally printed in Malaysia by Printmate Sdn. Bhd. (89371-D) 14 & 16, Jalan Industri P.B.P. 7, Taman Industri Pusat Bandar Puchong, 47100 Puchong, Selangor D.E.

1.

'Three rules of work: out of clutter find simplicity; from discord find harmony; in the middle of difficulty lies opportunity.'

Albert Einstein

Getting a promotion depends heavily on being noticed for positive reasons. So, whenever there is a problem, particularly if the difficulty is raised by management, then this is an excellent opportunity to get in the spotlight. Very importantly, you do not need to provide the solution, and you will not be expected to; but if you are prepared to put in the extra work to try things out, and are enthusiastic about trying different solutions, you will be in the management's favour. And if one of the solutions you're working on solves the problem, then there is a high chance you will share in the rewards. One deed alone may not result in a promotion, but it will certainly put you head and shoulders above the competition.

Getting Promoted. David Hirst

2.

'If A equals success, then the formula is A equals X plus Y and Z, with X being work, Y play, and Z keeping your mouth shut.'

Albert Einstein

In terms of getting promoted, if you have anything negative to say, particularly when it involves other co-workers, the management, or the company as a whole, keeping your mouth shut is essential. Voice only those comments and remarks that are positive, contribute to the task at hand, or offer alternative solutions for consideration. It is a generally accepted fact that management dislike people who whinge, even if they do so themselves on occasion. People generally feel more comfortable with other positive people and shy away from interacting with those who complain all the time. To get noticed, be positive and keep your mouth shut whenever you have anything bad to say.

Getting Promoted. David Hirst

3.

'Going to work for a large company is like getting on a train. Are you going sixty miles an hour or is the train going sixty miles an hour and you're just sitting still?'

J. Paul Getty

At the end of the day after a hard day's work, you may feel absolutely drained and completely exhausted. It may also seem that the company is doing well and progress is being made. However, you need to ask yourself if *you* are making progress too, both in skills development and career development – although one may compensate for the other, depending on your priorities. So, even though it seems that great headway is being made, you need to assess if this is really true for you, or it's just the company you work for. If it's just the company, then sit down and start making some career goals you wish to achieve, and make these known at your next staff appraisal/assessment, or even earlier if the opportunity arises.

Getting Promoted. David Hirst

4.

'Everything comes to him who hustles while he waits.'

Thomas A. Edison

If the workload eases a little, or there is a lull in activity, there is a tendency for staff to check their WhatsApp, social network sites, and gossip. Bosses know this and, in most cases, tolerate it – although some companies now limit internet connections. This quiet period is a perfect time to put in a bit of effort to clear a backlog of other work, or start a project that will get you noticed when completed. Many staff complain that they have no time to get involved in extra activities, but this is the excuse of a poor time manager. A good time manager recognises these pauses in direct activity and, instead of socialising with colleagues, they busy themselves with achieving above standard targets: they hustle while they wait.

Getting Promoted. David Hirst

5.

‘The only place success comes before work is in the dictionary.’

Donald Kendall

You have to work at promotion: it very rarely gets given to you. Perhaps the best place to start is to decide whether you are aiming for increased status, increased remuneration, or both. The former is easier as companies are usually quite willing to approve a different title providing it costs the company little or nothing in monetary terms. However, if it is both status and money you are after, it will take time, planning, and the application of hard work. Hard work alone is not the answer: it's the application of it that is the key. This requires your efforts to be noticed and appreciated. Put yourself in your bosses' shoes and think what would make a positive impression on them. Then work hard at it: the result is working smarter.

Getting Promoted. David Hirst

6.

'Hard work spotlights the character of people: some turn up their sleeves, some turn up their noses, and some don't turn up at all.'

Sam Ewing

One of the reasons that people avoid rolling up their sleeves and getting stuck in is that they tried it when they first joined the company and saw no immediate reward, so they considered it a waste of energy. The fact is, it's rare that hard work produces immediate rewards other than the intrinsic value of doing something well and achieving a positive result. However, over a period of time hard work gets noticed, and when management are considering promoting staff (perhaps so they don't lose them), then the hard worker will always be in with a better chance than those who are not. The smart hard worker even more so.

7.

'A chief petty officer taught me shorthand, which got me **promoted** *to yeoman first class.'*

Jack Adams

To help your chances of getting promoted, try and learn as much about the trade/business you're in as possible. Even if it's not directly related to your current scope of work, you will find that the information will come in handy should you look for a promoted post elsewhere as well as showing an interest in your current industry. It will show management you are committed to the company and that you are worth investing in as a future senior manager.

Getting Promoted. David Hirst

8.

'People are still willing to do an honest day's work. The trouble is they want a week's pay for it.'

Joey Adams

Unless you are running your own company, there will nearly always be a tendency towards sluggishness when you have the choice of working harder or less hard. And, generally, people always want more for their efforts than before. There may be very good reasons for this such as inflation, but the fact remains that if you want to increase your chances of a promotion, you will have to ensure, at a minimum, two things: do an honest day's work; and don't complain. Make suggestions, by all means, but make sure they're positive in nature for the company, not just for you.

Getting Promoted. David Hirst

9.

‘Don’t bite off more than you can chew.’

Proverb

Although many of the quotes so far are about getting noticed by putting in that extra bit of effort, it's worthwhile mentioning that you should only take on those extra jobs that you seriously think you can do well. If you are taking on extra work and then having to go back to management to explain why you haven't achieved a result or finished what you set out to, then it will reflect negatively on you. So the message here is be selective about what additional work you take on. Also make sure that it doesn't affect your success with your regular responsibilities. However, see the next quote as well.

Getting Promoted. David Hirst

10.

'The secret to my success is that I bit off more than I could chew and I chewed as fast as I could.'

Paul Hogan

It may seem as though this quote contradicts the previous one; however, what it's putting into perspective is that if you say 'yes' to something you've not done before, or take on extra work that you'll need assistance with, make sure you have access to the necessary information or people to help you do a good job. And don't be afraid to ask for help from management, you will usually find that they will be only too grateful that you've volunteered to help them out. So say 'yes' and bite off a little more than you have ever chewed before, but then, as Paul suggests, chew like crazy.

Getting Promoted. David Hirst

11.

'Your imagination is your preview of life's coming attractions.'

Albert Einstein

One of the key differences between those who are chosen for promotion instead of overlooked is the ability to *imagine* a better future. And this is a function of being proactive rather than reactive. The following table shows a few of the differences in what we say.

Reactive Language	Proactive Language
There's nothing I can do	Let's look at the alternatives
That's just the way things are	I can choose to do things differently
I have to do that	I choose to do that
I can't	I will try
I must	I prefer
If only	From now on
I wish I had	I will

To be more pro-active requires using your imagination to question processes and look for alternative solutions to problems. If you are reactive, you will find it difficult to make a difference, whereas a proactive person will be able to create a better future and also feel more in charge of their destiny.

Getting Promoted. David Hirst

12.

'The creation of something new is not accomplished by the intellect but by the play instinct acting from inner necessity. The creative mind plays with objects it loves.'

Carl G. Jung

L ooking at a problem from a work perspective will usually just lead to similar conclusions, and these will tend to be on the negative that it can't be done. However, if you consider that solving the problem is potentially your ticket to a promotion, or even better, your ticket to an improved standard of living, then you are more likely to stimulate your creative side. Similarly, if you can look at the processes and systems in your workplace and literally dream up a better way of doing things, and you then present this in a well thought out (initially brief) proposal, then you will have the management's attention. Even if your idea is not adopted, the fact that you've shown initiative will be influential to those people in a position to help you.

13.

'Adults are always asking little kids what they want to be when they grow up because they're looking for ideas.'

Paula Poundstone

Children have wonderful imaginations that can turn an ordinary cardboard box into a castle or a spaceship. However, as we go through the socialisation processes of school and work, we get a lot of our creativity disciplined out of us. The situation is much better now as creativity is seen much more as a useful tool in work and life than it ever used to be. Nevertheless, when you are searching for a new idea to improve a process or an object, never reject ideas because they are too childish: with a bit of tweaking here and there, they have the potential to be some of the best.

Getting Promoted. David Hirst

14.

'One of the symptoms of an approaching nervous breakdown is the belief that one's work is terribly important.'

Bertrand Russell

One of my core quotes for a good life. In your search for a promotion, you will need to work smarter and often harder than those around you; however, always make sure that you are able to manage your time well so that you have a great life-work balance. If you find that you are thinking of little else but work, then it might be time to take a step back and re-assess the way you are approaching the goal of getting a promotion. No sensible company will promote people who are burning out, or on their way to a nervous breakdown.

Getting Promoted. David Hirst

15.

'By working faithfully eight hours a day you may eventually get to be boss and work twelve hours a day.'

Robert Frost

Many workers in companies all over the world see the boss as having an easier time than them. They see the easy style of the boss – if they are good at their job, their clear desk, the fact they always have time to talk to their staff. The staff think, hey, I'd like that lifestyle too. But becoming the boss is not a way to reduce the workload; in nearly all cases it's a way to increase the workload; it's just that good bosses don't show it. Sure, a boss is usually paid to manage resources, which requires a different set of sub-skills, but it is almost certain that they will experience greater stress levels. Consider this very carefully against the rewards before you decide your next step.

Getting Promoted, David Hirst

16.

'My life, my career has been like a roller coaster. I've either been an enormous success or just a down-and-out failure.'

Judy Garland

When you reflect on your career path, even if it's not yet that long, you may think that this quote sums things up for you too. However, there are many grey areas that we tend to forget in the mists of time. But one thing is almost certain: you will not be successful each and every time. Think of getting a promotion as writing a report: you will never be able to write the whole thing perfectly the first time, which means re-evaluating the way you have presented your ideas and re-drafting. You will find that your path to senior management is not a smooth straight line. Realise this so that when the failures come, they are more manageable (see the next quote).

Getting Promoted. David Hirst

17.

‘I have not failed. I've just found 10,000 ways that won't work.’

Thomas A. Edison

Your attitude to failure is as important a concept as your attitude to success. Success is usually easy to handle since most people are happy. But dealing with failure is a true test of courage. Management will never expect you to be right all the time – it's a near impossibility – but they will be very interested in the way you handle failure. Will you blame others? Will you give up? Will you sulk, or any other of a number of negative character traits? Or will you maintain a positive attitude and rise above it, because this is what will impress those in power more.

Getting Promoted. David Hirst

18.

'I've missed more than 9000 shots in my career. I've lost almost 300 games. 26 times, I've been trusted to take the game winning shot and missed. I've failed over and over and over again in my life. And that is why I succeed.'

Michael Jordan

All of the most successful people in the world have had failures. The number of those failures may be much less compared with the rest of us, but they nevertheless fail on occasion. So if things don't quite go the way you expect them to in the workplace then you are in very good company. The difference between the successful people – the stars of this world – and the rest of us mere mortals is that the stars never give up and use the failure as an incentive to make it better the next time.

Getting Promoted, David Hirst

19.

'A good manager is a man who isn't worried about his own career but rather the careers of those who work for him.'

H. S. M. Burns

It is actually in your manager's interest to manage your career path for succession planning purposes, and it also makes them look good at their job too. To say that they aren't worried about their own career paths is perhaps a little optimistic in the real world, but it would be great to work for a person who is like that. In the real world there are, unfortunately, some bad managers out there and we have to deal with them as best we can.

Getting Promoted, David Hirst

20.

'There is an enormous number of managers who have retired on the job.'

Peter Drucker

Many managers give up on the job as soon as they reach the position they think will be as far as they can rise to. They make themselves as comfortable as possible and do the bare minimum to get by without getting into trouble. And this makes life very difficult for those who would like to make a career in the same company. Thankfully these people are moving on, although nowhere near fast enough for many companies and their staff. In this case you have to assess the situation and if you find that you have one of these people for a manager then you should consider either a sideways shift in the company, or moving to another organisation. You can also do everyone else a favour by mentioning the honest reason why you are leaving/considering leaving to senior management. You never know they may wish to keep you and retire the manager.

21.

'Asking "who ought to be the boss?" is like asking "who ought to be the tenor in the quartet?" Obviously, the man who can sing tenor.'

Henry Ford

Before promoting people in most companies, management will need to evaluate the value of you doing a good job in your current position versus your potential of doing a good or better job in a promoted post. The risk of you shifting companies if you are not promoted is also thrown into the equation. It is why many companies give staff much of the work of the promoted post to see how they get on before officially promoting them. So, rather than complain about the extra work, embrace it and learn how to do it well. Then, after a suitable period of time, you could broach the subject of balancing your new duties with an increase in grade and/or remuneration.

Getting Promoted. David Hirst

22.

'Don't blame the boss. He has enough problems.'

Harold Rumsfeld

Casting blame for mistakes, however accurate it may be, serves very little purpose. No-one likes to be blamed and pointing fingers at the boss is hardly likely to endear you to them for promotion. You can't change the past, but you can learn from mistakes so that you minimise the chances of the error recurring. If something is your fault, acknowledge it and move on to the better future. If it's someone else's fault, then just focus on the solution and the future.

Getting Promoted. David Hirst

23.

'Opportunity is missed by most people because it is dressed in overalls and looks like work.'

Thomas A. Edison

It is very unlikely that any promotion will be handed to you on a plate: you will have to earn it. Further, if you think that getting a promotion will make your life easier, well financially it might, but in all other respects probably not. It will mean a bigger workload, increased stress and more demands on your time. So, you can start getting used to this by seeing hard work as opportunities for advancement, not just hard work on its own.

Getting Promoted. David Hirst

24.

'*It is not titles that honor men, but men that honor titles.*'

Niccolo Machiavelli

It may be that your main drive for a promotion is title and status. In this case you will have to demonstrate to those who bestow such titles that you will honour the title, not the other way around. And this will require demonstration of a character that fits with the designation. It's no good saying that you'll change once you receive the title (or any promotion, for that matter), because they will simply not believe you and remind you that a leopard cannot change its spots. Demonstrate first, reward later.

Getting Promoted. David Hirst

25.

'I'm still at the beginning of my career. It's all a little new, and I'm still learning as I go.'

Orlando Bloom

This quote reminds us that you never really stop learning. After you get your promotion, a whole new world will open up requiring further learning. And this should be embraced. When you stop learning you are either dead or you have given up on life.

Getting Promoted, David Hirst

26.

'Don't waste time learning the 'tricks of the trade'. Instead, learn the trade.'

James Charlton & H. Jackson Brown, Jr.

Doing just enough to get by will never be enough, unless your goal is to use the job as a stop-gap until something better comes along. But if you are looking to be in the post for some time, then it is beneficial to keep learning. You never know when you might need to talk knowledgeably about the subject, especially if you have to attend a series of interviews for your next appointment and explain in detail what you've been doing.

Getting Promoted. David Hirst

27.

'There is no escaping the fact that, even in a great career, sometimes the best advances happen through luck, chance and accident.'

Edmond Fischer

S ometimes it seems as though things are destined
for us. If you look back on your career/life so
far, you would be forgiven for thinking that
both good and bad things have been engineered our
way for a reason. I'm not superstitious, but I do
believe in fate, and to ignore these coincidences can
prove costly. So always keep an open mind to ideas
and events around you, even if they don't initially
seem related to your goal of getting a promotion. They
still might, in some weird way, lead towards it.

Getting Promoted. David Hirst

28.

'If the career you have chosen has some unexpected inconvenience, console yourself by reflecting that no career is without them.'

Jane Fonda

Things happen. And for sure they are not always going to be good or beneficial to us. However, the way you deal with these incidences is a key indicator to Management of your potential. It's easy to enjoy the good times, but the person who will do well in a company (or on their own) is the one who can manage life's let downs well too.

Getting Promoted. David Hirst

29.

'I have gone from a player who thought he would spend his whole career with one organization to a player who's been with three organizations in a week. It's like rotisserie baseball.'

Mike Piazza

However hard you work, and however much you follow your boss's advice, and however many successes you achieve, you may still find that you are not getting promoted. In this scenario, you should give serious thought to looking elsewhere i.e. other companies, and preferably to a promoted post rather than a lateral move. Although moving companies too often is viewed negatively, you also have to balance this with the fact that it's in manager's interests to keep you where you are, especially if you are good at what you do.

Getting Promoted. David Hirst

30.

'Some of the best business and non-profit CEOs I've worked with over a sixty-five-year consulting career were not stereotypical leaders. They were all over the map in terms of their personalities, attitudes, values, strengths, and weaknesses.'

Peter Drucker

This is a wonderfully reassuring quote for most people as we really can't be exactly the same as our bosses. They may try and mould their staff into miniatures of them, but the reality is that we are all individuals with our separate personalities, hopes, ambitions and goals. When these match favourably to our boss's it usually results in a great working environment. However, good bosses support and exploit differences for the good of the task at hand or the company as a whole, so there is a lot of benefit to being different. After all, if we were all the same it would be a very boring place, wouldn't it?

Getting Promoted. David Hirst

31.

'What is it that you like doing? If you don't like it, get out of it, because you'll be lousy at it.'

Lee Iacocca

If you are thinking of moving to a promoted post but are not looking forward to the scope of work, consider first if you can change the scope of work at all. If not, move, learn the skills necessary to do a good job and then move on. You may even find that the work becomes more interesting as you discover more about it. Nonetheless, if you still find you don't like the tasks, the fact that you will be focussing on moving in the future, will help: it will remind you that it is just a temporary evil that you need to endure before moving on to greener pastures.

Getting Promoted. David Hirst

32.

'For many people a job is more than an income – it's an important part of who we are. So a career transition of any sort is one of the most unsettling experiences you can face in your life.'

Paul Clitheroe

etting a promotion also depends on your priorities. If you really love what you do, but the chances of getting a promotion are limited, than you have to consider the trade-off. Yet, in my opinion, until you've tried another job or company, you'll never really know if you would enjoy that even more. The mind will convince us that we are happy where we are because it really is stressful moving companies, making new friends and dealing with a whole new set of people. I say take the chance.

Getting Promoted. David Hirst

33.

'It is never too late to be what you might have been.'

George Eliot

I love this quote, because it reminds us that it is never too late to work towards a promotion. It's really just a concept shift. On the other hand, there are people who say they are very happy with their job and position. Yes, they would be happy with a higher salary, but essentially they are not the ambitious types. And this is fine, wonderful in fact. But make sure that you are truly happy as it is in fact never too late to aim for a promotion.

Getting Promoted. David Hirst

34.

'Sometimes you learn more from failure than you do from success, and in some ways it's better to have failure at the beginning of your career, or your life.'

Michael Crawford

It may not seem so at the time, but failure early on in your career is far preferable than later for the simple reason that you have more time to correct the mistake and/or start again. Of course, it does depend on the type of failure you make, but mistakes and failures will happen however much we try to avoid them, so learn from them and move on. Hopefully you will learn enough along the way to avoid them in the future.

Getting Promoted. David Hirst

35.

'Your Business clothes are naturally attracted to staining liquids. This attraction is strongest just before an important meeting.'

Scott Adams

Actually, a lot of what people think of us is decided by how we look. And there is one secret that can help you: always dress slightly – ever so slightly – smarter than your colleagues. If you are going to get promoted you will be expected to look the part, and management will want to see the potential of this before they make their decision.

Getting Promoted. David Hirst

36.

'Communication – the human connection – is the key to personal and career success.'

Paul J. Meyer

Communication is so important, yet people are often so bad at it. They don't listen, they don't ask the right questions, and worst of all they react to people based on what they think they can get away with. The most essential aspect is training yourself to be a good listener; the most critical is using emotional and social intelligence effectively.

Getting Promoted. David Hirst

37.

'Criticism of others is futile and if you indulge in it often you should be warned that it can be fatal to your career.'

Dale Carnegie

If communication is the key to success, then
criticism must be the key to failure. No-one likes
to be criticised and realistically it serves very little
purpose other than a cathartic effect for the
complainer. We all make mistakes and we can all learn
from them, but to dwell on past errors does not take
the situation forward. It's also very demoralising for
the people involved. So, whenever you want to
criticise someone for a mistake or being foolish, just
put yourself in their shoes for a moment and see how
you'd feel.

Getting Promoted. David Hirst

38.

'It is extremely unlikely that anyone coming out of school with a technical degree will go into one area and stay there. Today's students have to look forward to the excitement of probably having three or four careers.'

Gordon Moore

There are many differences between the younger generation – Gen Z and Y – and the management – Gen X. One of the more notable of these is that the attention span of Gen Z and Y people is much less. Before Gen X, people used to think of a job as a career for life; however, Gen X broke new ground by moving from one company to another to get promotion or simply to take their career in a different direction. Gen Y take this one stage further and *expect* to move; they also have much more freedom to choose and can adapt to new situations far quicker and more efficiently than their predecessors. Bosses are only now waking up to the fact that to keep their Gen Y staff, they are going to have to create interest, opportunity and diversity. It's becoming a very fast paced world.

Getting Promoted. David Hirst

39.

'A lot of fellows nowadays have a B.A., M.D., or Ph.D. Unfortunately, they don't have a J.O.B.'

Fats Domino

This is a lovely humorous quote that reminds us that you often need a formal qualification just to get your foot on the career ladder. There was a time, not too long ago, when all you needed to do was turn up for the interview and show willing. Now, for the same job you're expected to have a degree. And jobs that were available with a degree now require a higher degree. The message here is that we cannot afford to rest on our laurels as there will always be someone more qualified to take our place. Keep learning, both on the job and formally, and you will have every chance of success.

Getting Promoted. David Hirst

40.

'Don't worry about people stealing your ideas. If your ideas are any good, you'll have to ram them down people's throats.'

Howard Aiken

In all of the companies and industries I've worked in, there has been at least one person with a great idea on how to improve systems and processes in the company. And they are so protective of this idea that it never comes to fruition. They worry so much about other people stealing the glory of their initiative – often the boss they dislike – that they never voice it out. And this is a terrible mistake. Yes, the boss may take some of the glory, but they would be equally foolish to claim the idea as their own. My advice is this: present the idea to the boss, or if you really dislike them, then put it in writing to the senior management/HQ. Then follow it up to see if they like it and offer to be a part of implementing the idea. At the very least it would prove an interesting subject to talk about at a future job interview.

Getting Promoted. David Hirst

41.

'Setting goals is the first step in turning the invisible into the visible.'

Anthony Robbins

It may be a cliché, but it is always worth reminding ourselves that very little gets done without planning. It helps avoid procrastination and gives a beginning, a journey, and a destiny. If you want anything in this life, be it a promotion, a raise, a new career, you need to think how you're going to achieve it, because for sure it won't fall in your lap. Another cliché to support this is 'failing to plan is planning to fail'.

Getting Promoted. David Hirst

42.

'You can have everything in life you want, if you will just help other people get what they want.'

Zig Ziglar

As with all the best Zig Ziglar quotes there is an underlying focus, a heart, if you like, on the key to any individual's success being in the hands of the person you are dealing with. If you can show them you understand them and their position, they will happily work with you. If you focus solely on what you want, then the chances are that you will not achieve as much as you could have. Therefore, to get a promotion, first understand things from the boss's perspective. if you were the boss, what would you require of someone before you promote them? And therein lies your answer.

Getting Promoted, David Hirst

43.

.

*'If you think your boss is stupid, remember:
you wouldn't have a job if he was any
smarter.'*

John Gotti

A wonderful quote that highlights the fact if you think you are smarter than your boss, make them feel good, because they are likely to be grateful to you. Be thankful that you are smarter and can therefore do something about your career much easier than if they were smarter than you.

Getting Promoted. David Hirst

44.

*'All that is human must retrograde if it does
not advance.'*

Edward Gibbon

If you are working in a company and do not have a career plan, then there is a very high chance you are retrograding or, at the very least, not progressing. It is an absolute waste of opportunity if you fail to progress. You can take small steps at first such as picking up a book to motivate yourself, or ask management to attend a training programme. From there you should have some ideas of what to do next. If you're still in doubt, get another book and attend another course.

Getting Promoted. David Hirst

45.

'Restlessness and discontent are the first necessities of progress.'

Thomas A. Edison

Being contented usually means being happy with the status quo, but the wonderful irony with us human beings is that as soon as we achieve it, we look for something else, something better. We get bored with the same and seek variety in our lives, which we then try to conquer so that the variety becomes less challenging and more manageable. Then, as soon as this happens, we take a moment's reflection and search for something new. As the quote suggests, it is often that it is the boredom with what we have that makes us move on to better things.

Getting Promoted, David Hirst

46.

'Work while it is called today, for you know not how much you will be hindered tomorrow. One today is worth two tomorrow's; never leave that till tomorrow which you can do today.'

Benjamin Franklin

It is very easy to make excuses and put off applying for, asking for, or working towards a promotion. There's always tomorrow, but when tomorrow comes it will still be easier to not do anything than commit to a plan of action. Why wait? Is it the fear of failure, the fear of change, or perhaps the fear that your colleagues may notice you are choosing a different path to them? The latter is more common than people openly admit. The herd instinct is very powerful and encouraged in companies through teambuilding activities and company events. To get a promotion it will mean standing out from the crowd, and for some that is a high price to pay; however, I can assure you it is worth it.

Getting Promoted. David Hirst

47.

*'One must work and dare if one really wants
to live.'*

Vincent van Gogh

If you take the decision to make a determined effort to work your way through to management, and you work with a number of co-workers, there will initially be some resentment. Your fellow workers will sense competition, and even more significantly, they will see the potential of their own future in the company take a step backwards. You must therefore dare to be different and resist their attempts to bring you back down to their way of thinking.

Getting Promoted, David Hirst

48.

'The ancient Romans had a tradition: whenever one of their engineers constructed an arch, as the capstone was hoisted into place, the engineer assumed accountability for his work in the most profound way possible: he stood under the arch.'

Michael Armstrong

One of the key things that impresses management is the ability to take responsibility, as it's one of the essential elements of being a good leader. A manager's responsibility is not necessarily being able to do the job better than anyone else, it's the ability to take responsibility for the work that's done, and to guide the process so it conforms to the company's ideal.

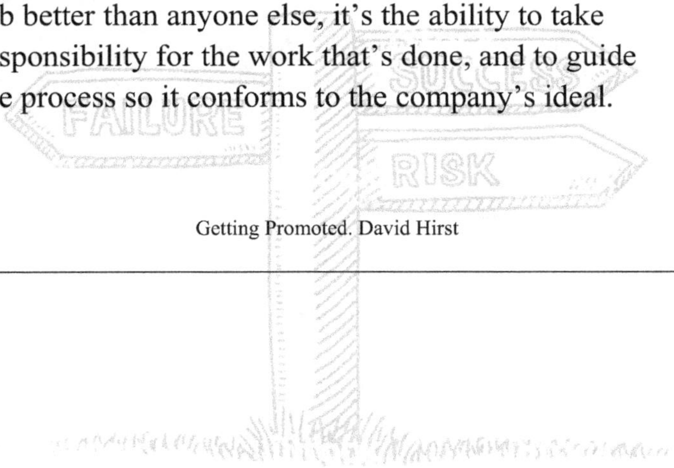

Getting Promoted. David Hirst

49.

'The people who get on in this world are the people who get up and look for the circumstances they want, and, if they can't find them, make them.'

George Bernard Shaw

Knowing what you want in this world is more than half the battle to having a good life. After deciding on a career, obtaining the position you would like to be in the company within a specific time frame requires the presence of certain circumstances. These could be a favourable boss, the opportunity to become involved in a successful project, or being noticed at the time of a special achievement, or any number of things that your promotion requires. Sometimes, however, circumstances don't favour us and we have to go out and make them. For example, if you don't have a favourable boss, then move to another department where there is one, or to another company; create a special project; report your achievements – modestly and realistically; and so on. Waiting for the circumstances to be right may mean they never happen at all.

Getting Promoted. David Hirst

50.

'A dollar picked up in the road is more satisfaction to us than the 99 which we had to work for; and the money won at Faro or in the stock market snuggles into our hearts in the same way.'

Mark Twain

The idea of getting something for nothing is a
lovely idea. The only problem is that it rarely
happens. Friends will boast about the good
deals they get, but almost never the bad. However, the
fact remains that if you want to get a promotion, you
are going to have to work for it. Sure, there will
always be one lucky individual who appears to get
promoted without effort, and it makes the rest of us
feel left out. Why can't we have the same luck? And
so there are those who decide to wait for their luck to
turn in their favour. And that would be a mistake,
because more luck comes to those who deserve it than
not. In other words, working hard for a promotion is
also the smart thing to do. If your luck changes along
the way then it's a bonus.

Getting Promoted. David Hirst

51.

'Let the world know you as you are, not as you think you should be, because sooner or later, if you are posing, you will forget the pose, and then where are you?'

Fanny Brice

Ultimately you have to be yourself as there is no way that you can maintain the pretence of being someone else forever. If you are required to work in teams but you are just not cut out for that, irrespective of whatever training you receive, then recognise the fact and use it to your advantage by applying for jobs in departments that require a lot of working independently. Conversely, if you are better suited to teams and like working with people, then seek those jobs out. To get a promotion you will have to excel at what you do, and that will be almost impossible if you are pretending to like tasks that deep down you hate. Recognise what you are and like doing and communicate that.

Getting Promoted. David Hirst

52.

'Starting out to make money is the greatest mistake in life. Do what you feel you have a flair for doing, and if you are good enough at it, the money will come.'

Greer Garson

This follows nicely on from the previous quote. The main message is that you are less likely to succeed at things that you are not passionate about. There must be drive, or desire to do what you do. And communicating that enjoyment and passion is more than half the way forward to getting a promotion as you will naturally do the job well and with a positive attitude. If you are pretending, people will notice that too and you should consider a sideways shift to something you think you would enjoy before aiming for a promotion.

Getting Promoted. David Hirst

53.

'There are costs and risks to a program of action, but they are far less than the long-range risks and costs of comfortable inaction.'

John F. Kennedy

U nfortunately, too many people leave it too late to really explore their potential. So many could have risen to manager, senior manager, director and so on, but because of inaction, failed to do so. One of the reasons for this is that they fear the unknown consequences of doing something different from their co-workers, but it is precisely this that will get you noticed. Further, you may not always be successful, but the amount you learn from your mistakes far outweighs any disappointment.

Getting Promoted. David Hirst

54.

'The unknown is what it is. And to be frightened of it is what sends everybody scurrying around chasing dreams, illusions, wars, peace, love, hate, all that . . . Accept that it's unknown, and it's plain sailing.'

John Lennon

This is the big mental wall to overcome: the unknown. Children are not actually frightened of the dark; they are frightened of what evil things may lurk in the dark. It is also the same concept with adults in the workplace; they are not frightened of the change, but of the unknown evil things the change may bring. I find it interesting that the focus is often on the negative (evil) things rather than the positive benefits and opportunities. All change brings opportunities in one form or another, so embrace change and accept that there will always be the unknown to it, then you can move on to the opportunities the change brings.

Getting Promoted. David Hirst

55.

'Many men go fishing all of their lives without knowing that it is not fish they are after.'

Henry David Thoreau

Everyone around you will expect you to get a promotion at some stage in your career. Your family, in particular, will have very high hopes for you. And so you try your best to get promoted and work your way up the corporate ladder. However, the vast majority are also thinking along the same lines. Therefore, one of the first questions you need to ask yourself is whether a promotion is what you really want. Or is it actually to satisfy those around you more. If it truly is what you are looking for then starting to make the changes necessary for it to happen will be so much easier.

Getting Promoted, David Hirst

56.

'The difference between a job and a career is the difference between forty and sixty hours a week.'

Robert Frost

One of the key changes you will probably need to make is to accept that to get a promotion you will need to work for it, as very few are handed to you on a plate. This will also impinge on your social and family life to the extent that you may have to re-consider your current lifestyle. For sure, to keep your current lifestyle and think that you can just add more hours at work is avoiding reality. It will be very much worth it, and provided you have communicated why you are making these changes, will usually be supported.

Getting Promoted. David Hirst

57.

'Keep away from people who try to belittle your ambitions. Small people always do that, but the really great make you feel that you too can become great.'

Mark Twain

Another major change you will probably have to make is who you spend your time with. There will be those people who are jealous of what you are trying to do with your life, and rather than them trying to do something with theirs, they would rather see you fail. They will be negative about your efforts and try to persuade you that your endeavours are a waste of time. Try and mix with those who support the energy you are putting in. These positive people are usually the ones who are successful themselves and will want you to enjoy the joys that success brings too.

Getting Promoted. David Hirst

58.

'A man wrapped up in himself makes a very small bundle.'

Benjamin Franklin

While you need to concentrate your energy on getting a promotion, you also need to be aware of your surroundings. You may still be part of a team that needs your support too; you will also need to ensure you still maintain as balanced a lifestyle as possible; and you also need to keep check of how the extra work may be affecting your relationships with others. At the end of the day, a promotion on its own is a very lonely thing unless you have someone to enjoy the success and the benefits with.

Getting Promoted. David Hirst

59.

'The closest to perfection a person ever comes is when he fills out a job application form.'

Stanley J. Randall

I really like this humorous quote that reminds us that people can be very creative when it comes to job applications. Just bear in mind that you may be expected to live up to the claims. In fact, the closer you can get to living your job application, the closer you will be to a promotion. And when you can exceed it, you will get it.

Getting Promoted. David Hirst

60.

'We pretend to work because they pretend to pay us.'

Anonymous

This is the main excuse that people use to avoid working hard and putting in extra effort. However, there's another expression: 'invest in loss to gain', which I find more realistic. In other words, you have to put in the hard work first before you get the rewards. And I've found this statement true of pretty much everything I've ever achieved.

Getting Promoted. David Hirst

61.

'Desire! That's the one secret of every man's career. Not education. Not being born with hidden talents. Desire.'

Bobby Unser

Contrary to many educationalists out there, and speaking from personal experience, I agree 100% with this quote. The desire, the passion, is crucial, and the education can come later. A good education is very useful and a great help in understanding the machinations of life. However, a person with a great education may not necessarily be the most successful. A person with desire will. The best, of course, is to have both.

Getting Promoted. David Hirst

62.

‘The first and best victory is to conquer self.’

Plato

To add to the previous note on desire and education, I would like to add a third crucial element for career success: self-discipline. It's always very easy to make excuses for not doing those things you promised to yourself you would, and to make excuses for putting off the goals you've set for yourself. However, if you want the promotion, the career success, then exercise self-discipline. By all means reward yourself upon completion of the task, but conquer yourself and keep up the self-discipline.

Getting Promoted. David Hirst

63.

'We all have dreams. But in order to make dreams into reality, it takes an awful lot of determination, dedication, self-discipline, and effort.'

W. Jesse Owens

Absolutely! There is rarely an easy path to take, and if there is, you usually only find it while applying the above. Achieving success only appears easy after you have applied these principles and you look back on what you have accomplished. Then you have a choice: to tell everyone that it was an easy journey for you or that it required determination, dedication, self-discipline, and effort.

Getting Promoted. David Hirst

64.

'An unfulfilled vocation drains the colour from a man's entire existence.'

Honore de Balza

How terrible the words 'I should have' or 'I wish I had'. It is a great shame that so many people say them when they are nearing the end of their careers. Time appears to go so slowly when youth gives the impression that there's so much of it; and as middle age creeps in, how much faster it disappears. So, the message here is find your vocation and fulfil it. There is not always a tomorrow.

Getting Promoted. David Hirst

65.

‘This is the best result in my career up to now.’

Sofia Arvidsson

The key words in this quote are 'up to now'. Hopefully, as you get promoted or get near to achieving whichever goal you have chosen, you will see a new path, or a new goal that motivates you to even greater achievements. If you ever stop challenging yourself, you are giving up on life. Yes, there may be times you need to stop, smell the roses, and enjoy the rewards of your efforts, but there should always also be an excitement about what the future holds.

Getting Promoted. David Hirst

66.

'My career is going better now than when I was younger. Now I get the part. Back then, I'd get the girl.'

Michael Caine

Age often makes it easier to get promoted, although less so these days. As companies move more towards meritocracy rather than seniority structures, it is becoming much easier to have younger people in senior positions managing older staff. It has never been easier for hard work to pay off. Previously, you could put in all the sweat, but not get promoted because of age constraints. Now results matter more than ever, and now is the time to make the most of these changes.

Getting Promoted. David Hirst

67.

'To play with Zinedine Zidane was the biggest honour I have had in my career.'

David Beckham

As you progress through the company or through companies, always remember to be humble with your achievements. By promoting the virtues of others, you are also promoting yourself, but in the nicest possible way. And people respond to this well. If you are leading a team and the team does well, look to highlight the good in others as this adds to your qualities as a manager.

Getting Promoted. David Hirst

68.

'Working with Ronnie Barker was always a joy and were without doubt some of the best years of my career.'

David Jason

Wherever you rise to in your industry, the real joy of where you get to is only vindicated by your enjoyment of the job and the people you work with. Promotion on its own has very little meaning without being able to share the success and get pleasure from the new challenges you face. Determination is an essential aspect of career success, but it is people who make the fun in life.

Getting Promoted. David Hirst

69.

'It's not what you achieve, it's what you overcome. That's what defines your career.'

Carlton Fisk

Every job, whatever you do, brings problems and aggravation. It's how you handle these issues that helps you on your career path. Even if people unrealistically expect you to be right every time, they will forgive errors, because even if the expectation is there, the reality is there too. Nobody's perfect.

Getting Promoted. David Hirst

70.

'If you're a careerist, thinking only to advance your media career, then I don't really want to work with you.'

Michael Moore

Although it is good to let your managers and bosses know that you are intent on a career with the company, it is also very important to ensure that it does not determine your only reason for being there. If it is, then your co-workers will quickly tire of your company and view you as selfish. Have fun, learn, and offer to help others with things that matter to them.

Getting Promoted. David Hirst

71.

'My mother said to me, "If you become a soldier, you'll be a general, if you become a monk you'll end up as the pope." Instead, I became a painter and wound up as Picasso.'

Pablo Picasso

An essential part of getting a promotion is to have confidence in yourself. Your family and close friends will support you, but the key to making things happen is to believe in you. There is a clear distinction between arrogance and confidence and make sure you fall into the latter's category. Give people in the workplace the excuse to believe in you too.

Getting Promoted. David Hirst

72.

'There is no security in life, only opportunity.'

Mark Twain

When you get the promotion you've been looking for, be careful not to start thinking that you can take it easy and cruise through the job: it doesn't work like that. As Mark twain states 'there is no security', so you need to make sure that you re-set your goals and make a plan of action to increase your value to the company. Even if your security is not assured, make it stable enough for you to enjoy your life to the fullest.

Getting Promoted. David Hirst

73.

'More men are killed by overwork than the importance of this world justifies.'

Rudyard Kipling

Go for the promotion, but keep things in perspective. It is most certainly not worth ill health, even for a short period of time. Stress is a silent killer: it creeps up on you when you think things are still under control. A typical reply to the question 'Are you stressed?' is 'No, I'm fine.' Some people are more susceptible to the effects of stress than others, and you need to keep an eye on your stress levels to ensure that when you get the promotion, you are fit and healthy enough to fully enjoy the rewards it brings.

Getting Promoted. David Hirst

74.

'*I have always argued that change becomes stressful and overwhelming only when you've lost any sense of the constancy of your life. You need firm ground to stand on. From there, you can deal with that change.*'

Richard Nelson Bolles

When you are promoted, it will often require changes to your life, especially at the early stages. And this is likely to result in increased levels of stress, particularly as your colleagues may treat you differently now you are a higher grade than them. The best way to deal with this stress, in fact any stress, is to make sure that you have constancy in a balanced lifestyle. For most people this will relate to your home and family life. Work on this as hard as you work on getting a promotion, so that when it comes you will be better prepared for any changes.

Getting Promoted. David Hirst

75.

'So I was in my car, and I was driving along, and my boss rang up, and he said 'You've been promoted.' And I swerved. And then he rang up a second time and said "You've been promoted again.' And I swerved again. He rang up a third time and said 'You're managing director.' And I went into a tree. And a policeman came up and said 'What happened to you?' And I said 'I careered off the road.'

Tim Vine

I've included this as a last quote because above everything else in your quest for a promotion, keep a sense of humour, otherwise it will all be for nothing. You have to enjoy what you do for the most part, and also enjoy (again, for the most part) the people you work with. If you feel this is not possible, then you should look to gain your financial independence in another company or line of work.

Getting Promoted. David Hirst